D1074794

# ARIZONA
## A PICTURE MEMORY

**Text**
Bill Harris

**Captions**
Laura Potts

**Design**
Teddy Hartshorn

**Photography**
Colour Library Books Ltd.
FPG International

**Picture Researcher**
Leora Kahn

**Commissioning Editor**
Andrew Preston

**Editorial**
David Gibbon

**Director of Production**
Gerald Hughes

CLB 2874
© 1992 Colour Library Books Ltd, Godalming, Surrey, England.
All rights reserved.
This 1992 editon published by Crescent Books,
distributed by Outlet Books, Inc., a Random House Company,
40 Engelhard Avenue, Avenel, New Jersey 07001.
Color separations by Scantrans Pte Ltd, Singapore
Printed and bound in Singapore
ISBN 0 517 07266 1
8 7 6 5 4 3 2 1

# ARIZONA

## A PICTURE MEMORY

**CRESCENT BOOKS**
NEW YORK · AVENEL, NEW JERSEY

Until air conditioning made it practical for people to thrive in the Arizona climate, it was generally regarded as a place that had to be endured on the way to California. Some men, of course, wanted to be there for there was gold and silver enough to make a man rich, and copper in abundance. Others were there in spite of themselves. In the 1870s, nearly a quarter of all the men in the United States Army were stationed in the Arizona Territory, in places with such infamous names as Fort Apache and Fort Defiance, and few of them were pleased to be there When one optimist among them suggested to his commanding officer, General William T. Sherman, that it wasn't such a bad place and that all it needed was better people and more water, the General snapped: "That's all hell needs."

The Indians, including the Apache and their cousins the Navajo, along with the Pima and Hopi and others, thrived there, and even today there are more native Americans in Arizona than in any other state. And the land has always been hospitable to all sorts of plants and animals. The saguaro cactus, for instance, whose flower is the official symbol of the state, has a life expectancy of some two hundred years. Other plants encourage further forms of life. The yucca, which grows in dozens of different varieties, needs moths to pollinate it, and it returns the favor by giving life to more than thirty different kinds of moths that couldn't survive anywhere else. And not all the creatures native to Arizona are like the kangaroo rats that actually run from water when it's placed near them. The first Anglo-Americans who moved into Arizona were trappers in search of beaver skins, and the descendants of the animals they missed are still at work in the high country, damming streams and creating ponds.

There are hundreds of different kinds of animals that find Arizona a perfect place to live, including many that are unique to to the area. But some have man to thank for their home. When elk became extinct there, a herd of Roosevelt elk, a species more at home in the Northern Rockies, was driven down into the Arizona mountains, where it has expanded to the tens of thousands. Bison, which were never indigenous, were introduced into Arizona about a century ago and, although there are only a few hundred in the state today, they seem content to stay. Not every attempt to improve on Arizona wildlife, however, was such a success. Consider the camels, for instance.

After the Mexican War in 1848, the Mexican president Santa Anna ceded the territory north of the Gila River, including most of Arizona, to the United States. The following year gold was discovered in California and the route across the new territory was the quickest way to the riches, but the terrain was rough. It was too rough to build a railroad, which was the obvious answer, and Congress authorized James Gadsden to buy 30,000 square miles south of the river from the Mexican president to give the Americans an easier right of way. But what really interested them were mineral rights, and because of the rush to dig gold, silver, and copper in the new territory, the railroad was a long time coming. In the meantime, there was still a transportation problem. But Congress, even back in those days, wasn't short of bright ideas.

With very little debate, the conferees appropriated the necessary funds to send a delegation to Turkey to buy a herd of camels and recruit a few good men to handle them. The beasts and men arrived in Arizona in 1856 ready for work. It seemed like a good idea at the time, because each of the camels, the "ships of the desert," was able to carry more than a quarter ton of freight about fifty miles a day. They could walk for days without water, and whatever happened to be growing along the side of the trail was more than enough for them to eat. Like many other newcomers to America, the camels ran into prejudice every step of the way. Admittedly, they aren't much to look at; they have strange voices and it is often hinted that their breath might just be fatal. On the other hand, the competition was mules and they are hardly the sort of animal that inspires great paintings and heroic sculpture. In fact, it's difficult to imagine the love Arizonans expressed for their mule teams when the debate turned to the relative merits of mules versus camels for desert transport. Every mule train that crossed the desert had to include a complement to carry food for them, routes had to be mapped with frequent water holes in mind, and valuable time was almost always lost because the animals' feet were often torn by the rocky terrain. In an effort to settle the argument, a camel enthusiast challenged the mule skinners to a contest to carry a two-ton load for sixty miles. It took six camels two-and-a-half days to do the job, whereas twelve mules, hauling the same load, needed four days to cover the same ground. But even that didn't convince anyone. The camels, they said, frightened the mules. They probably scared quite a few of the men, too. At any rate, the experiment was given up as a bad job and the camels were retired. Some were sold at auction in California and Nevada and others were simply turned loose, and all the camel drivers but one went back home. The one who stayed was named Hadji Ali, but most folks called him Hi Jolly and, possibly as a sign that all was forgiven, when he died in 1902 he was buried under an elaborate pyramid in the cemetery at Quartzsite, the only monument to the experiment that lured him to America. But there are no monuments in Arizona to another creature that was transplanted from the other side of the world and gave cowboys something to think about for thirty years around the turn of the century.

In the 1890s, no fashionable woman considered herself properly dressed without ostrich feathers as part of her costume. The cost of importing them from Africa made them uncommonly expensive, but they were, after all, a necessity, and as a service to the fashion conscious, Arizona ranchers began raising ostriches. It made a lot of sense to the cattlemen because the average ostrich needed about four pounds of feed each day compared to the fifty needed for a steer, and a full-grown bird was worth three or four times as much as a longhorn. Profits could also be increased by shearing feathers during the time it took the big birds to reach maturity. Ostriches, however, turned out to be more ornery than camels and mules, and when the fashion changed ranchers were just as happy to go back to the beef business, while most of the ostriches they had nurtured were quickly converted to fertilizer.

The steers that made Arizona attractive to cowboys were also among the animals introduced by man, as were the horses that helped them do their job. The cattle were descendants of longhorns left behind when Spanish rancheros were driven out by the Indians and of strays from cattle drives on their way to California to feed the forty-niners. Though the Anglos didn't get around to serious ranching in Arizona until the mid-1850s, the horses the Spanish brought had been at work changing human life there for more than three hundred years.

Ironically, the ancestor of the horse evolved in the Colorado Plateau, which runs across the center of modern Arizona, about 100 million years ago. Before the evolutionary cycle was quite complete, however, the creature migrated across the land bridge at the northeast corner of the continent into Europe and Asia, and it ceased to exist in North America not very long before man began crossing the same land bridge headed the other way. There is evidence that those early wanderers found their way to Arizona as many as 12,000 years ago, and by 3,000 B.C. they had established an advanced civilization that included sophisticated irrigation systems, and an urban culture whose people lived in multi-story cliff dwellings long before European cultures thought of the idea.

By the time the Spanish arrived looking for golden cities in the 1530s the old cultures had vanished, and only the ruins of what they had created remained. The natives they found, with very few exceptions, were newcomers themselves. Most of them were farmers and hunters and, until the horses the Spanish brought began to change their lives, all of them were tied to the land. Many of the tribes, the Hopi and Navajo for example, kept their old ways, but others became the best and most formidable horsemen the world had seen since the Mongol hordes terrorized the steppes of Western Asia.

It was the Apache who drove the Spanish vaqueros out of the Southwest, and they were such an elusive enemy that no one felt safe from them. Their warriors were able to cover a hundred miles a day once they had horses, and they were masters of striking silently and suddenly and then disappearing without a trace. The Spanish and Mexicans endured them, but were never able to stop them, and when Americans began crossing Arizona during the California gold rush, the U.S. government, deciding it had a responsibility to protect its citizens, began building a string of forts across the territory.

The American soldiers were no match for the wily Apache, who were made more irritable by the presence of silver mine boom towns and the encroachment of cattle on the open range they considered theirs. The soldiers, however, had the advantage of guns, and once the braves realized it was futile to challenge the horse soldiers to battle they turned to the tactics that they knew best: stealth and guerilla warfare.

The soldiers managed to subdue the other tribes and relocate them on reservations, but the Apache eluded them for more than twenty-five years, during which time their great chiefs, Geronimo and Cochise, kept up the pressure that made life a chancy proposition in the Arizona Territory. The first real breakthrough came in an unpredictable way when Thomas Jeffords established a mail route across territory dominated by the Chiricahua Apache. There was nothing especially outstanding about Jeffords, but he impressed Cochise by riding into his camp unarmed looking for permission, and the old chief allowed the mail to go through. A few years later, when General Oliver Howard suggested that the whites and Indians should bury the hatchet, Jeffords was instrumental in the negotiations. Cochise agreed to peace on two conditions, firstly that the Chiricahua should keep its land as a reservation and secondly that Jeffords would be the Indian agent.

One reason why Cochise didn't want to be moved was that the reservation was a perfect base for raids into Mexico, and, when the chief died, the government decided to take away the advantage by moving them further north. Naturally, the Indians weren't too pleased, and it took nine columns of cavalry to convince them. But it didn't end the war. Unscrupulous Indian agents added insult to the injury of the move, and Geronimo and forty of his braves led 5,000 cavalrymen on a fruitless chase across the Southwest. At one point, the soldiers endured three weeks of hard marching, following elusive clues, only to discover that Geronimo had led them in a great circle and they were less than thirty miles from where they started. It was another two months before they found him or, rather, that he allowed himself to be found.

Tired of running, Geronimo's band encouraged him to surrender and, once captured, he and his people were sent to Florida as prisoners of war. Along with them went Apache scouts who had served alongside the horse soldiers, including ten who had earned the Medal of Honor, America's highest award for bravery. As far as the white man was concerned in the 1880s, there were "good injuns" and "bad injuns," and most believed that the only good ones were dead ones.

Not all the whites were what one would call "lily-white." Though when Wyatt Earp arrived in Tombstone in 1880, he brought what passed for respectability in the person of his brother, Virgil, a deputy to the U.S. marshal at Tucson, he was also in the company of some rather disreputable characters. These included his other two brothers and John ("Doc") Holliday, a former dentist who found gambling more to his liking than pulling teeth, as well as Luke Short and Bat Masterson who, in addition to being handy with cards, were accomplished writers and knew a thing or two about manipulating the press. They had come from Dodge City, where Wyatt was a deputy sheriff, and all of them had been successful gamblers. Tombstone was a rich mining town where the so-called Dodge City Gang expected to cash in at the gaming tables, and Wyatt was determined to become sheriff of the newly-formed county, a job that had all sorts of money-making possibilities, from the protection money paid by saloon keepers to a generous share of the taxes that the peace officer collected.

Wyatt Earp didn't get the job, but together the Dodge City Gang managed to get its share of enemies among members of a local gang of cattle rustlers led by "Old Man" Clanton and his three sons, who had had the town to themselves before the newcomers arrived. The feud started when Clanton and five of his men were killed by Mexican smugglers, and Wyatt used the incident in his campaign to be appointed sheriff. It was intensified when the Earps led a posse to capture the perpetrators of a stagecoach holdup that might just, depending on which side is to be believed, have been committed by Doc Holliday. And it came close to boiling point when Virgil became city marshal and offered Ike Clanton a bribe to implicate some of his own gang members in another stage robbery. Not long after Ike refused the offer, Virgil arrested him on the street for possession of a pistol and beat him with the offending weapon all the way to the jailhouse. The same day, Wyatt also pistol-whipped Tom McLaury for riding his horse on the sidewalk, and as McLaury led his mount over to the O.K. Corral the feud was ready to boil over.

The gunfight that followed is one of the most famous of all the stories of the Old West, but no one knows for sure what really happened. What is known is that McLaury was the first to be hit, and before he died he seriously wounded Virgil; and that all of the Clanton gang was dead in less than thirty seconds. Thirty-four shots were fired, and of the rustlers' seventeen bullets, three hit their mark, wounding Virgil and his brother, Morgan, and grazing Doc Holliday. Wyatt Earp walked away untouched, even though in his own account he said that he never ducked for cover. In the aftermath, the local judge released them all on grounds of insufficient evidence.

Cattle rustlers and stagecoach bandits, crooked marshals and fierce hostile Indians are as obsolete in modern Arizona as camels and ostriches. When it became the forty-eighth state in 1912, the last of the so-called Continental United States, the American Frontier disappeared forever. As if to emphasize the change, when President William Howard Taft signed the paper that made statehood official, the event was recorded on motion picture film, the first, but hardly the last, time a president became a movie star. And the new governor, George Hunt, went to the capitol building in an automobile. There were plenty of cowboys firing their six-shooters at the sky, but the grand finale to the celebration, a forty-eight-gun salute, was stopped abruptly after the thirty-eighth salvo because the concussion was breaking windows in Phoenix and giving the horses a terrible fright.

In the decades since statehood, Arizona's pioneering spirit has drifted into high-tech industries, its towns have become sprawling cities and Arizonans tend lawns on what was once a desert and relax in backyard swimming pools in places that get little more than three or four inches of rain a year. But the Wild West is still out there, in a landscape that ranges from the windswept Sonoran Desert to the wonders of the Grand Canyon and the rock formations of Monument Valley, where the air is so clear it is possible see landmarks fifty miles away, any day.

Yet there is more to Arizona than wind- and water-carved rocks and vast deserts. About twenty percent of the state is covered with forests that include more ponderosa pine than any other state, as well as stands of bristlecone pine that are well over a thousand years old. Oranges grow in valleys sheltered by snow-covered mountains and the desert blooms with lush farms and cotton fields, many of which owe their existence to irrigation canals.

The ancient Indians used such canals to carry water to their cornfields, and in the 1860s an entrepreneur named Jack Swilling cleaned out the old system and began promoting farmland near the Salt River. Where there are farms, towns often follow, and the one that grew up around Swilling's development soon had everything but a name. Swilling, a veteran of the Confederate army, wanted to name it for his hero, Stonewall Jackson, but in a spirit of democracy he formed a committee to debate the subject. An orator among them put everyone to sleep with a long-winded speech about new civilizations rising from the ashes of ancient ones, and by the time he reached the climax by suggesting that it should called Phoenix no one was in a mood to object and the name became official. Twenty years later, when it became the capital of the Arizona Territory, its name seemed quite appropriate. It was, after all, the site of the oldest civilization in the place that became the United States, and it was the last of the Continental territories to make a contribution to the American mosaic.

*Montezuma Castle (facing page), a magnificent twelfth-century structure, is built into the cliff face over 100 feet above Beaver Creek, in the Verde Valley. It was built by the Sinagua Indians – rather than by the famous Aztec king as its name suggests – when a severe drought forced them into an area with a reliable supply of water. The five-story, twenty-room building is one of the best-preserved cliff dwellings in the country and is a National Monument.*

*Monument Valley (below and bottom right) covers 29,816 acres of the Navajo Reservation and stretches across the border between Arizona and Utah. The valley has a beauty of its own, with magnificent sandstone buttes, shaped by erosion over the centuries, characterizing its arid landscape. Since 1959, Monument Valley has been a Navajo tribal park (right). Center right: the White House Ruins, Canyon de Chelly National Monument, in the Navajo Reservation.*

*Lake Powell (below) is the work of man rather than of nature. The spectacular lake, the fifth and newest of the reservoirs on the Green and Colorado rivers, was created in 1963 when the newly-completed Glen Canyon Dam (center right) was brought into operation. Navajo Bridge (bottom left) spans the Colorado River as it makes its way through Marble Canyon. Left: the plains at Bitter Springs. Overleaf: rugged scenery southwest of Page.*

The Grand Canyon (these pages) is one of the seven natural wonders of the world. From Moran Point (above) and Yaki Point (center left), on the East Rim Drive, the views are spectacular. The landscape below Mohave Point (below and facing page bottom), a popular observation point on the West Rim Drive, reveals the stark beauty of the Canyon. Top left: views around the Watchtower. Bottom left: Bright Angel Trail. Facing page top: the landscape below West Rim Drive. Overleaf: a vista of the canyon from Hopi Point Lookout.

*Lake Havasu City (this page) is a tourist resort. London Bridge (below and top right), its principal attraction, was bought by the town's founder, Robert McCulloch, in 1968, shipped from London, and reassembled in its original form over a man-made channel of the Colorado River. The resort boasts fine hotels such as the Queen's Bay Hotel (bottom right), as well as a golf course (right). Facing page top: the Hoover Dam. Facing page bottom: boats moored at Lake Mead Marina.*

21

Coconino National Forest (facing page), in north central Arizona, boasts some spectacular scenery, ranging from deep canyons and gorges, to rolling landscapes and forests. On its northern boundary stand the magnificent San Francisco Peaks (below). From the summits of the peaks, which at 11,600 feet are the highest in Arizona, there are breathtaking views of five states. Right: the Granite Dells near the town of Prescott, in central Arizona.

Oak Creek Canyon (below), in Coconino National Forest, is famed for its colorful rock formations. Of these Cathedral Rock (right) is perhaps the most renowned. Its richly-colored spires, which tower above the surrounding landscape, are reflected in the waters of Oak Creek. The town of Sedona (center right) is situated at the southern end of Oak Creek Canyon. Bottom right: land around Beaver Creek. Overleaf: Oak Creek at Red Rocks Crossing.

*When construction of the village of Tlaquepaque (above, top left, bottom left, and below) – an arts and crafts village near Sedona – was begun in the autumn of 1971, it was the realization of Nevada businessman Abe Miller's dream. Nearby Jerome State Historic Park (left) chronicles the history of Arizona's mining past. Facing page top: Montezuma Castle National Monument. Facing page bottom: Arcosanti, a "city of the future," near Cordes Junction.*

The Painted Desert (below), east of the Grand Canyon, stretches across much of northeastern Arizona. The vibrant colors that inspired the area's name are found in the layers of sandstone, shale and clay, rather than in vegetation, which grows sparsely on the arid plateaus and buttes. Petrified Forest National Park (center left and bottom left), covering 94,189 acres of the Painted Desert, contains an extensive collection of petrified trees. Left: Meteor Crater near Winslow, formed by a falling meteorite over 22,000 years ago.

The views of Apache National Forest, in east central Arizona, from Highway 666 (below) are dramatic. The highway follows the contours of the Mogollon Rim, a rugged escarpment over 1,000 feet high that stretches across the eastern part of the state, dividing it into two. The east fork of the Black River (center right and bottom right), like many of the forest's lakes and rivers, offers fine trout fishing. Right: a view across the landscape towards Springerville.

Tonto National Monument (facing page), near Theodore Roosevelt Lake in south central Arizona, was set up in 1907 to preserve one of Arizona's unique archeological sites. The remains of the cliff dwellings built by the Salado Indians between A.D. 900 and 1350 provide a unique insight into the pattern of their lives. Left: a view of the Salt River. Below: the Highway 60 Bridge spanning the Salt River at Salt River Canyon in San Carlos Indian Reservation. Overleaf: Superstition Mountains, east of the Mesa, at the Gateway to the Valley of the Sun.

Phoenix (these pages), the sophisticated capital of Arizona and cosmopolitan heart of the southwest, retains the Spanish, Indian, and American West influences that originally shaped it. Sleek, modern high-rises such as the Valley Bank Center (facing page) on 1st Street, and the Hyatt Regency Hotel (below), on Phoenix Civic Plaza, stand side by side with older buildings such as St. Mary's Church (top right and bottom right), and the 1912 State Capitol (right). Overleaf: an aerial view of Phoenix.

*At night the bright lights of Phoenix (below), the ninth largest city in the United States, stretch almost as far as the eye can see. Innovative sculpture by Arizona sculptor John Waddel on Phoenix Civic Plaza (center right and bottom right) is lit at night, bringing magic to the heart of the city. Right: Old Scottsdale – 5th Avenue shops at dusk.*

*Below: the leisure center, near Scottsdale Mall. Scottsdale, a large and fashionable suburb of Phoenix centered around Old Scottsdale, was chosen by the famous architect Frank Lloyd Wright in 1938 as the western center for his studio and school. This choice added to the area's reputation as a center for artists and crafts people. Facing page top: an aerial view of Scottsdale. Facing page bottom: the town of Prescott, the one-time state capital, in central Arizona.*

*Beyond the colorful vegetation (below) rise the shadowy forms of the Pinaleno Mountains, in Coronado National Forest. The scenery in the forest reflects the diversity that is characteristic of southern Arizona's landscape. Catalina State Park (center left and bottom left), north of Tucson, borders Coronado National Forest. The rugged Santa Catalina Mountains form a magnificent backdrop for the park. Left: Gates Pass, to the west of Tucson.*

Tucson (these pages and overleaf) was one of the first Spanish settlements in the West, and reminders of this heritage still abound in the modern city. Mission San Xavier del Bac (left), poetically known as the "White Dove of the Desert," is perhaps the best-known of the city's ancient buildings. The present building dates from 1782, though the mission itself was established in 1700, and is still used by the Papago community. Tucson's Pima County Court House (facing page and below) was built in 1928, in the Spanish Colonial Revival style. Overleaf: a view of Tucson, from Sentinel Peak, which has been nicknamed "A" Mountain.

Old Tucson (these pages), situated twelve miles outside of Tucson, was originally constructed for the film "Arizona" in 1939, and has subsequently been used as a location for numerous films and advertisements. Since it was opened to the public in 1958, Old Tucson has been immensely popular. A variety of recreational activities are on offer, including the Simmons Gun Museum, frontier train rides, and gun fights on Front Street.

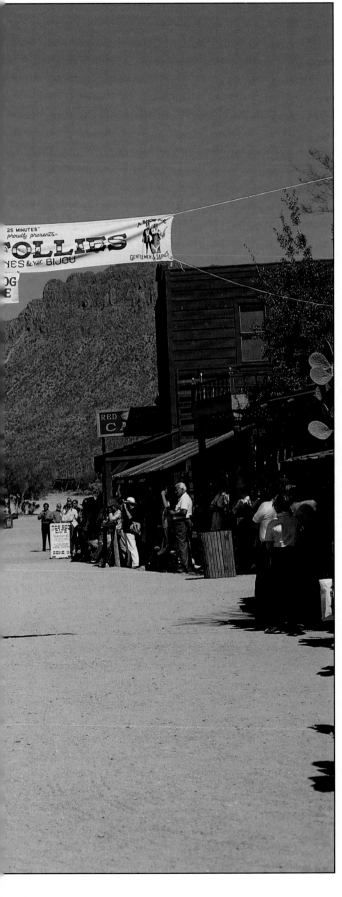

There are few things that are more beautiful than the desert in flower. Above: giant saguaro cactus. Below: totem pole cactus. Top right: organ pipe cactus. Right: prickly pear, beaver tail cactus. Bottom right: golden barrel cactus. Facing page: saguaros at sunset. Overleaf: giant saguaro cacti, in Saguaro National Monument.

Tombstone (below, left, and facing page), a prosperous, nineteenth-century mining town, was almost legendary in its lawlessness and deservedly holds a special place in the myths of the West. The town is now a National Historic Site, and many of its buildings, including the Tombstone Courthouse (below) have been fully restored. Above: the Pinal County Building at Florence. Top left: Kitt Observatory. Bottom left: Mission San Jose de Tumacacori, north of Nogales.

*Organ Pipe Cactus National Monument (these pages and overleaf), covering 500 square miles in southwestern Arizona, preserves the natural beauty of the Sonoran desert. The organ pipe cactus from which the national monument takes its name is just one of the many cacti that flourish in the park. Following page: Prieta National Wildlife Refuge, Arizona.*